New & Selected Poems
(1984 - 2011)

Also by Cliff Burns:

The Last Hunt (2012)
Eyes in the Sky (novelette) (2011)
So Dark the Night (2010)
Of the Night (2010)
Righteous Blood (2002)
The Reality Machine (1997)
Sex & Other Acts of the Imagination (1990)

New & Selected Poems
(1984 - 2011)

Cliff Burns

BLACK DOG PRESS

Cover Design: Chris Kent

Interior Design: Daniel Middleton of Scribe Freelance

Published by Black Dog Press (blackdogpress@yahoo.ca)

Author website: http://cliffjburns.wordpress.com

ISBN: 978-0-9694853-6-0

Some of these poems first appeared in the following publications: *Freelance, The California Quarterly, The Timber Creek Review, Poetry Motel* and *languageandculture.net*.

for my sons

Early poems

Shadow Dweller

Fear the light
for it illuminates
the horrible creatures
that have crouched unseen
all these years.

Darkness can be a comfort,
sometimes.

(*1984*)

from *violins in the void*
(1985-1995)

Olduvai

left to their own devices
the progeny
in small sullen bands
stumbling naked
pursuing the burning sun

　　　—herds scattering
fearful of these bent-backed apes
　　　cruel and arbitrary
　　　　　as new gods

excreted
laboratory preserved
thawed
sprinkled over fertile ground
thriving like wild weeds
in unspoilt gardens
tended by inexplicable hands

2:00 a.m. (Crib Death)

Mutant baby cries
ululating prehistorically otherworldly

Will the Japanese dispatch a mini sub
charge exorbitant rates,
prospective researchers and groupies
trolling the depths of the borrowed crib
taking flannel soundings,
investigating promising results
for signs of life

Babytalk

No words can convey
I am reduced to this
thick-tongued
nasal love consonants
neolithic gutterals
quieting primal fears
taking the dark off the night

The Child Killer

Behind all the others, finally,
a death's head mask
of pale, ashen calm
and lips as dry as a desert moon;

the eternal spook
sniggering in your childhood closet
and rustling under your dreaming bed.

Shadow Puppets

fingers enacting exotic shapes
menacing silhouettes
tender to the touch

Fond memories of an excellent provider

The night shutteredbolted

small whitefaced mice fiercebeating hearts
throats clutched minds frozenimpenetrable

...and the immortal unkillable father
prowlingcreeping somewhere out there
beyond the kitchen door:

his babies *still* tucked and waiting
in grownup, shivering beds

It! The Terror From Beyond Space

taking on the shape of the father
huge and menacing when the zipper doesn't show
clawed fingers/horrid burning eyes
feasting on my crewmen one by one

W.C.B. (Rest now.)

I only knew my father as an old man
whittled down by life
a soul yearning to be reborn.

Dad was a consummate victim of larger forces
and intelligent enough to know it;
a symbol of rage and impotence
mean and racist and tragic
terrible and fearful and doomed.

Patriarchy

They want to put the blood back into the rituals; they
want to unsheath the sacrificial knives; they think our sons
have grown soft and decadent; they are firm, even severe,
but claim to punish in the name of love.

All men are monsters
their creations and motivations monstrous
the only saving grace:
built-in obsolescence

      i.e. a dead man's switch

a biological silver bullet
already in flight

Westerlies

The wind has teeth and it has eyes and it has
a voice a raw cancerous roar and it senses
the slightest weakness cuts you out of the herd
kills with the skill of a Serengeti lioness;

because all winds originate in the Dark Continent,
ancient whispers from Olduvai.

Exoskeleton

Precious bones
scattered on blistering sands
wind ablated
hot to the touch

The scavengers were cloaked
hooded
faceless;
ulna tibia fibula femur
tucked in burlap
grating like broken pottery

Filed and polished
fluted intaglio
the American woman
brazen in face and manner
paying inflated dollars
posing before the dirty mirror
my teeth grey and calcified
against her pale throat

fragment from a poem never written

…and you enlisted shadows
to aid your deliberate plans
demanding obeisance
without once showing your true face

Never to be seen again

> lost in the Bermuda Triangle
> burnt up with the shuttle astronauts
> bailing out with Amelia Earhart
> sharing a joint with Elvis

No smoking guns
no traces
just a hole in the universe
where a person used to be

Martians

The last known traces of a dissolute species.

Brutal artifacts
of a million year old crime scene
exposed to the light of day.

(Insectile eggheads chittering,
disputing cause and effect.)

Requiem

This poet is obsolete
his presence no longer required
scorned by those living in denial
of the metaphors and rampant symbolisms
gnawing on the guts of the body politic;

gritty realism resists his efforts
at imposing rhyme or reason
the hustle and bustle demanding a *vérité*
the mere page cannot impart;

his death rattle a gabble of syllables
too esoteric to be deciphered
by soundbitten minds
tabloided to stupefaction
greeting card sensibilities...
alliterative headlines proclaiming
dog and pony shows for the post-literate.

to let my fears speak for themselves
either figuratively or literally
to give them complete license
the freedom to express
to always hold close the imperative
"forgive all thoughts and deeds"
to attempt new insights
without old rancors
the looking glass of history
a pin through my thorax
excavations on my spirit

Ha'nt

They accumulate

                                        (the moments)

    first in dusty corners
    a sense of perpetual clutter

then suddenly underfoot

                                   like a scurrying grey cat
turning 'round and 'round
brushing up against ephemera
      smelling you on my clothes
      tasting you on my fork

tantalizing presence

                                      (essence)

    in my most secret rooms
each morning offering fresh evidence
of another discreet visitation

Adultery

Withhold nothing
but endure my evasions and lies;

whispering your rival's name
with my last shivering breath;

my soul willingly ceded
the signature unmistakable;

ugly and feral and shrewish
everything you are not;

neurotic and jealous and demanding
drawing my fingers to her lips;

straddling me
and entering me;

The song we sing
the notes wrung from me
dissonant to resentful ears

Theory Of Everything

How many cubic physicists
can you fold into an irrelevant universe
without running afoul of Newtonian absolutes
baked into shortbread cookies?

Monster

There is nothing that cannot be achieved
through sustained effort and an exertion of the
will; the mind can bend and shape reality at its
discretion; *while sleeping, I murder the world.*

buddha protect me
from Old Testament gods
& their psychotic tantrums
& sacrificial sons
& contradictory texts
& dim-witted acolytes
& literal mindedness
& Armageddon dreams

Sunday *(Day 7)*

My last waking thought
a heresy,
ghastly in its implications:
a loophole not closed
a singularity to bedevil perfection

I will not burden you with a title
leaving you nameless and faceless
like a creature out of Beckett
enduring despite the hastening void

from *Redbook, Volume I*
(1996-2006)

Magritte

I've never trusted my senses
I know sometimes looks can deceive
perspectives thinly receding
a marked absence of ceilings

en de lux

it was night
all over the world
empty, barren thresholds
cooling hearths
evidence of hurried departures
trampled grass and running feet

Blackbird

There is no music in the crow's heart
    not for him the aimlessness of bright birdsong
    the vacuity of colorful plumage

his raucous laughter at the very idea

I am fearful of the gifts you bring
square boxes secured with deft ribbons
damp and spongy on the bottom
where something has soaked through

Talisman *(compulsively)*

put this where it won't
get lost, some place
you visit
regularly
to
reassure
yourself against
those voices that insist
nothing is real

Some Assembly Required

the face in the upstairs window
invalid child who will never run
jump, play ball, make love (or war)

Broken or, rather,
unfinished
set aside
left to dry

the places we've known
entire neighborhoods inside us:
rows of like houses
half-forgotten rooms
long, chill corridors
surreptitious footfalls
stirring but never shifting
sedimentary layers of neglect

so tired of being stupid
playing catch-up
needing to have things explained to me

you'd think by now I would've learned
no further life lessons required
be like everyone else I know
& squeak by with a passing grade

Urbano Sapiens

mutant strain
evolutionary dead end
marked for extinction, leaving
a scatter of interesting bones

Atlas, shrugging
(for Stacey)

Of burdens insupportable
a crumble, a wreck
a shell of your former self

You were no longer you
the deception would not hold—
imagine waking from a nightmare to a nightmare
the toll that would take

I'm not saying that was an adequate excuse
what's broken can be fixed;
you were good with your hands
and should have known that

Unforgiven

your death a rare act of selfishness
that you never once looked back
or paused to say "good-bye"

In Memoriam

If the suffering has ended
why does pain still live here?
The impulse to scream, break the incessant silence,
exult a sorrow too long held in abeyance.

Blue Poles

a family murdered in innocent beds
cowering against the approaching slaughter...

investigators unnerved by the ferocity of the crime scene
all the postmodern touches
including a stream of consciousness rant
too obscure to be divined
gorestained onto soft white walls
of still rooms, in abhorrence of everything human

the Greeks, naturally, had a word for it
denoting an all-consuming rage
even vengeance could not slake;
they revered and feared it
named it as you would a daemon or malign spirit
celebrated in ritual and song
sating it with the iron blood of the valiant
to win favor for their warrior race

Atê

fists clenched   teeth bared
      liquid guts
the *stink* of acidic shit:
this is what has been given you
in lieu of Paradise
for services rendered

the dread come creeping
invisible voices conspire
nattering chorus of the incorporeal
jeering my every word

run
a long way
tell them I am coming
(whisper it as though you are afraid)

Woodsman's Disease

deliberately wandering from the path
following the river course
doubling back to foil the search party
until all hope is lost

Lump

You are all that's left
having eaten the rest of me
from the inside out
'til nothing remains.

Now, poor cancer,
you're lonely, suffering for companionship
cursing the thoughtless fragility
of your former host.

Useless

this futile hate
cannot move mountains
or bring down governments
or summon fire from the sky...
it churns in my violent guts
undigested meat by-products
ground and pulped
bilious excrement
the stench of frustrated conceit

Status Quo

I spit at you
kick and scream
act up in public
libel you with gross words
stabbing long after the body is dead

sinister forces aligning
the evidence plain to see—
cryptic messages in the *Personal* columns
secret looks on compromised streets

Sex (Copernican Style)

Above your sweating head in the holy east, Cygnus
    June-blooming, nightflowering in dark matter

while with quick-erratic breaths on the verge of becoming vowels,
your sharp, tangy musk redolent of outlandish alien shores

space is filled with color
gorgeous pinks, violets and blues
billowing from exploded suns
delicate wisps of membranous nebulae
a billion shades of black
spreading in all directions
to far distances, measured in time
dazzling birth/death throes
broadband and recorded as promising blots

God = Newtonian order
God in every quanta
God of the micro/macro scopic
God in the details
God, the master artisan
Of love and Auschwitz
Creator and destroyer
Shiva and sphinx
God of space and time
God in me jealous of the God in you

surrender do not contest the
will of a Creator who persists
despite science despite reason
cling to irrational belief/faith
the God of wonder I embraced
as a brilliant child

Lon Chaney

of my thousand faces I confess
this is the one I like best

Lon Chaney, Jr.

Taking any part they offer me
mugging with Abbot & Costello
stiff jolts of rye whisky
to endure the wolfman makeup
remembering dear old Maria Ouspenskaya
her sad and gypsy eyes

Lagrange

held at arm's reach
drifting never closer
too far to touch
dim point of mirrored brilliance
a flicker on the periphery of sight

Natural Selection

tidal nudges/
salt tropic waters/
overflowing with life/
spilling onto heavy shores/
suffocating by the *trillions*

long elegant beasts
rest thick matted heads on
exaggerated forepaws
stirring from their midday torpor
only when ground tremors describe
the passage of grey heedless behemoths

specious deity
leaving the lights on like that
now look what has grown
under your careless sun

St. Anthony's Lament

There are places even here in the desert
where I can hide from myself.

New Poems

(2007-2011)

Mass Extinction

It feels like the end of something
a dead zone spreading outward
from some remote Pacific atoll

I remember when the weather was normal
and the bees weren't dying
and you could see the stars

Since when did the natural become *un*-natural
man-killing winds
biblical floods
the grass eating holes in our shoes?

And who will feed all the hungry mouths,
Mother,
if you take sick and wither away?

Bouquet

Remember, thou art mortal
as doomed as a spring flower.

Shine brightly in your scant time
a dazzle of colors until you are plucked.

"Darkness, take my hand"

Here come the shadows
here they come
watch them come
come shadows
come shadows
here they come
here they come

21st Century Blessing

To a future effulgent:
tall trees and new flowers;
give us our daily bread
and save us from the blight

Thine and thy kingdom
withheld from us 'til death;
keep them close, our sons and daughters
and protect us from the blight

Have faith in the miraculous
harbingers of grace;
conjure us sweet loaves and fishes
and save us from the blight

arcanum arcanorum
("secret of secrets")

those places you withhold
from everyone else
intimate folds
moist, dusky precincts
swells and ticklish bits
only I have known

Bird

"When that love was done with, I was left like a bird on a branch. I was no longer any use for anything." Paul Eluard & Andre Breton, *The Immaculate Conception* (Translation by Jon Graham)

I am that bird/a useless, futile *thing*/purposeless and unblinking/stiffly clutched on my shivering perch

Denied foresight, stratagems/creature of instinct, heedless/as scattered petals or blown seed/no decisions, save alarm and flight

> like the lilies of the field
> like the trees and stones,
> or a worm, turning in thick, black dirt

Free from striving and strife/charged only with existence/descended from dinosaurs/small-brained and tuned to the stars

Waking you with piercing melodies/disdainful of the tardy dawn/spying with small, beady eyes/as you depart for work in a funk

Nestled against the weather/high up where the cats can't reach/alert, yet lightly dozing/untroubled by what you call "dreams"

Boxes

They have departed to the pleasure domes
abandoned their husks to decay.

Meatless, eternal, every wish fulfilled.
Etheric couplings, satisfaction guaranteed;
high adventure, simulated to the last pixel
experience without significance,
vouchsafed by an overcautious A.I.

You can never die and so
you can never live
and virtual love is no love
at all.

They can mimic everything except a soul
(but you know it's only a matter of time).

December

I sing praises of December
(the Reaper)
smothering snows
suffocating cold.

Calling crows announce
the death toll overnight:
That which walks a frozen land,
passed by and left its cruel mark.

Deluge

"see my tears drop down again",
as over-burdened clouds
release their precious bounty

I knelt in the forest
waiting my turn,
just another drop of rain

Note: the first line is a direct quote from one of the survivors of the Khmer Rouge atrocities, responding to the lenient sentence meted out to a notorious torturer.

Eoster

for Sherron

Never too old for miracles
never so secure in my faith

Counting my blessings each morning
kissing them to sleep at night

There are trees to shade us
food to feed us
vistas for our eyes

The invention of color
the use of light
(*glory! glory! glory!*)

In praise of stars and flowers
tipping my face to the rain

Follow the trail of laughter, find me
poised between heaven and earth

Like the first bird that flew
into your welcoming sky

Forever and Ever

I think of you often and passionately—
in bright of day
or shaded by night,
interludes of vivid recollection

Distance does not impede
nor experience divide;
in this world or the next,
tomorrow and forever

Holy of Holies

immanence is one of those words
like *numinous*, like *YHWH*, like *love*
which belies the notion
that what is named
cannot be imbued
in a single, uttered sound or
invoked by spellbinding letters

Pyramid Lake, Jasper National Park
(July 29, 2010; 3:15 p.m.)

Cupped in a bowl
of rust-colored fingers
sun-glazed and cedar-breathed
becalmed by a lake
that can't make up its mind
if it's blue or green...

And there's you, at the end of the dock,
slow-rocked by intrauterine swells
skin pinkening
in the magnified light
despite my frequent reminders,
the way I fret over
your unchangeable ways.

Reaper

November is *bleeding*,
leached of color, vitality,
the land losing its life's blood
in dark, spreading gouts.
Anemic, brittle, desiccated
tiny bones crackling underfoot:
this is the graveyard of autumn.
Brightening it with festive lights,
disguising it with tinsel, false cheer
but unable to defeat the oppression,
looming like a storm front.
Hibernation is a state between life and death,
a sleep from which some animals never wake...
another hard winter descends from the mountains,
the sun creeping back to make way.

Salacious

When they put it like that
the emphasis/
angle/
slant/
you can *sort of* see what they're saying
and know something ain't right.

Leaks
rumors
unnamed sources
muddying the water
casting heedless stones.

A bloodless coup, flawlessly executed
save for a shriek from the machinery,
something living caught in the works.

Vow

Because I love her
and because I am an article of her faith
I will not betray her
today.

Because she is good and kind
and I cannot bear the notion of hurting her
I will not betray her
today.

Because her soul has never known darkness
and she does not wish to be acquainted with horror
I shall not betray her
today.

Because of her eyes and a smile
that insists all futures are bright
I must not betray her
today.

Last of your kind

you are a rare bird
lovingly preserved
caged against harm

Space Madness

I've been up here too long,
starting to imagine things:
voices aft
(where I let the air out)
noises from the hold
(where I put them afterward).

Iconic

(for Neil Armstrong)

The First Man must be humble
yet self-possessed in times of crisis
confident, as one who's been sorely tried.

Drop him, spin him, shake him
race his heart,
see if he dies.

Undaunted by fame,
puzzled by all the fuss,
natural in the glare.

Stick him in a close compartment,
sling it into the girding dark;
crown him with hero's laurels
should he return.

No worlds, but one

More than anything else
we should be compelled &
transfixed by *wonder*.
This world is,
statistically speaking,
a miracle and for all
its implausibility,
might well have been
conceived and created
by a sentient, doting God

SPF

Night skies are deadly,
lit by a billion boiling stars;
radiation, invisible
and lethal,
malignancies that take eons
to kill.
Stars are not projectors
they are *suns*. Keep your
head covered, stay inside
on nights when it's clear.

Act of God

singular life
never to be exactly repeated;
a billion trillion simulations
and they *still* can't get your smile right

Foley Artist

You could hear bird song
incongruous, but it was there
ambient chatter
shrill commentary
from the safety of the trees

Away

My flesh craves
will *never* abjure
those pleasing symmetries
where our bodies meet.

Higher Physics

two souls
innately bound
strange attractors
destined to meet
fated to love

Burnt Offerings

I rebuke myself for inconstancy,
failing to carry the light.
My timid, convenient faith,
hastily abandoned, quickly reclaimed.
I mouth the ritual words,
follow along in the proffered hymnal,
but the *meaning* is lost.
My spirit dull-witted, malformed,
cowering from the gifts I am offered.

Metaphor

The 20th Century is a *skull*
gleaming in a dry creekbed.
Emaciated goats graze nearby
while, high overhead,
the sun sets fire to the sky.

No sound but the wind,
the awful, inescapable wind.

The Human Genome Project

They decoded us, then
trademarked the parts.
In green, tended tanks,
suspended in nourishing brine.
Eyes, ears. Kidneys. Small, bobbing cocks:
replacements for factory fittings,
ersatz and not nearly as smart.

By order of the President

Find the reagent
break the spell

There's still an outside chance
in your secret lab

Pls. advise on yr. progress
time is over and out

Morris Ankrum

you could see the wires
stars hung off-kilter
Earth just a rubber ball
a funny shadow where
someone lurked, just out of frame

Those of us...

who dream in slow motion
and have leaky prostates
and try so fucking hard
and who succeed, often in spite of themselves
and who have no mother or father
and who combat fear and depression
and who find ourselves inexplicably loved
and who are thankful for each blessed moment
and who know some day it must end

100:1

in miniature rooms
furniture built to scale
stiff, painted figures
coiffed hair, handmade clothes

placed with faces averted
subdued, for the sake of the kids;
a scandal in Smallville,
plastic lawyers on their way

Liar

Blameless only in deed.

My conscience accuses
and I concede.

Weak in the flesh
subject to evil thoughts
sinning in my heart like a whore.

Household God

In our prayers
& songs of devotion
By our deeds, with the
hands you've given us
Humble servants to one who is
infinitely distributed
while remaining ever present

Fragments & Apocrypha

I

at the tone, the universe
will be 13.7 billion years old

II

Is the paranoid mute tormented by whispering hands?

III

We move like elegant fish through pale, green
waters, always wary of sharks.

IV

I am a mage, a medicine man, shaking my bones
and banging my drum, while over the horizon the
machine civilization crouches, poised to leap.

V

SWM (non-smoker) seeks nice girl of independent means
and nurturing nature able to cope with intermittent
breakdowns, self-doubt, insomnia, erectile dysfunction &
premature hair loss. *Serious inquiries only*.

VI

I am weak, craven,
cowering before the scythe

VII

the fanatic has a relatively simple task
since failure is not an option

VIII

window:
an escape hatch
eight stories high

IX

I look for meaning wherever I can find it
torture it from reluctant witnesses
impose it by sheer force of will

X

Do you accuse God of killing out of malice?
Are you a blasphemer, deserving nothing but the stake?

XI

show and tell:
standing in front of the entire class
humiliated by empty hands

XII

where's the tough guy now
the Bogart I thought I was
the Cagney I aspire to be

XIII

watching your torturer's hands
so expressive, like a deaf person
signing an elaborate greeting

XIV

each breath a gift
each day a blessing
tomorrow a promise not necessarily kept

XV

Are you a liar, with an idolatrous heart
secretly worshipping false demigods
when you should be casting your gaze far higher?

XVI

in divine accord
like a flock of birds
wheeling & turning
wingtip to wingtip
tuned to the same frequency

XVII

to cultivate forgiveness
heal my itinerant soul
bestowing blessings
upon those who've wronged me
tactfully ignoring the knives in my back

XVIII

each day sees another loss
thinning ranks further reduced
besieged in my last redoubt
protecting my loved ones like sheep

XIX

memories of a feral childhood
dismissive clouts and nips
stealing scraps from siblings
surviving even if they must die

XX

It doesn't matter
something tells me the world will go on anyway
the ponderous ocean doesn't heed
nor will the ravaged moon abide

XXI

my approximation of a life
devoid of incident
programmed, set on automatic
existing wholly within the confines
of a pocked, hairless skull

XXII
(for Sherron)

inexplicable
like one of those miracle cures
your potent medicine
administered by loving hands
taking immediate effect

XXIII

dance like David
in heedless exaltation
drunk on the colors of Creation
every leaf transmuted to gold

XXIV

greeting a new morning
decanting the day
into a bright, clear vessel
rimed with dew

XXV

Time is accelerating
I can tell from the red shift
the speed you're moving away from me

XXVI

gazing up
you fall into it
the night, forever

XXVII

All is lost.
We're in here, waiting.

XXVIII

These are the last words I will ever write.

Afterword

by Cliff Burns

Even after all these years, I still struggle when trying to explain or summarize my approach to poetry, the "aesthetic" (or what have you) that informs structure, meter, syntax, etc.

In truth, I've never had much confidence in my verse. What I consider concise, spare, *compressed*, many others find terse, elliptical, even incoherent. And when pressed to elaborate on certain works, I find it well nigh impossible to offer anything worthwhile or insightful in response, my vague, evasive answers only serving to further muddy the water.

I rarely submit my poems for publication—part of it is fear of rejection, certainly…but there's something else too. My poetry unsettles me. To *me*, it's utterly revealing and offers an extraordinarily unflattering depiction of the state of my soul. The Void ever present, a pall of oppression and despair hovering over almost every poem.

Poem…isn't that the wrong word for most of these offerings? Aren't they more like mantras or chants or, yes, *incantations*? Ominous drumbeats from the id, some ancient place inside me, a cavern dimly lit with candles made of animal fat, reeking of blood and viscera. No gods, no spirit world, just proto-humans with Model T brains and a gift for tool-making. And killing.

There should be more light in this book. Most of the time I'm a happy, well-adjusted guy. Married, with children.

Blessed with robust health. I want to be a man of faith and retain at least the *possibility* of hope. For the sake of my loved ones, in opposition to chaos, heedless fate and random chance.

We do not live only to suffer. That would be inconceivable. We are higher order animals and demand more of our Creator.

We reward divine favor with fanatical devotion and will endure any pain, indignity or torment to serve a God we believe to be kind and just. Call it a sacred covenant. A promise made long ago we pray will never be broken.

April, 2012

Cliff Burns is the author of a number of books including *The Last Hunt*, *So Dark the Night*, *Of the Night* and *Righteous Blood*. His work has been adapted for the radio and stage and featured in numerous anthologies and publications around the world. He lives in western Canada with his wife, Sherron, and two sons, Liam and Samuel.